For every Black life, every Black hope, every Black dream
—C.B.W.

For my Grandpa C. D. Williams—because you talked
—F.C.

Grateful acknowledgment to Hannibal B. Johnson, author, attorney, consultant, and chair of the Education Committee for the 1921 Tulsa Race Massacre Centennial Commission, for reviewing the text and sharing his expertise.

Back endsheet photo: This June 1921 photograph shows the total devastation of the Greenwood District in the aftermath of the massacre.

Text copyright © 2021 by Carole Boston Weatherford
Illustrations copyright © 2021 by Floyd Cooper

Carolrhoda Books®
An imprint of Lerner Publishing Group, Inc.
241 First Avenue North
Minneapolis, MN 55401 USA

For reading levels and more information, look up this title at www.lernerbooks.com.

Photos are courtesy of the Library of Congress (historical), Floyd Cooper (family photo), and Danielle Carnito (Reconciliation Park).

Designed by Danielle Carnito
Main body text set in Aptifer Slab LT Pro Semibold.
Typeface provided by Linotype AG.
The illustrations in this book were created using oil and erasure.

Library of Congress Cataloging-in-Publication Data

Names: Weatherford, Carole Boston, 1956– author. | Cooper, Floyd, illustrator.
Title: Unspeakable : the Tulsa Race Massacre / Carole Boston Weatherford ; illustrations by Floyd Cooper.
Other titles: Tulsa Race Massacre
Description: Minneapolis : Carolrhoda Books, [2021] | Audience: Ages 8–12 | Audience: Grades 4–6 | Summary: "Celebrated author Carole Boston Weatherford and illustrator Floyd Cooper provide a powerful look at the 1921 Tulsa Race Massacre, one of the worst incidents of racial violence in our nation's history" —Provided by publisher.
Identifiers: LCCN 2020020949 (print) | LCCN 2020020950 (ebook) | ISBN 9781541581203 (trade hardcover) | ISBN 9781728417387 (eb pdf)
Subjects: LCSH: Tulsa Race Riot, Tulsa, Okla., 1921—Juvenile literature. | African Americans—Violence against—Oklahoma—Tulsa—History—20th century—Juvenile literature. | Greenwood (Tulsa, Okla.)—Race relations—History—20th century—Juvenile literature. | Greenwood (Tulsa, Okla.)—History—20th century—Juvenile literature. | Tulsa (Okla.)—Race relations—History—20th century—Juvenile literature.
Classification: LCC F704.T92 W43 2021 (print) | LCC F704.T92 (ebook) | DDC 976.6/8600496073—dc23

LC record available at https://lccn.loc.gov/2020020949
LC ebook record available at https://lccn.loc.gov/2020020950

Manufactured in the United States of America
1-47319-47946-8/26/2020

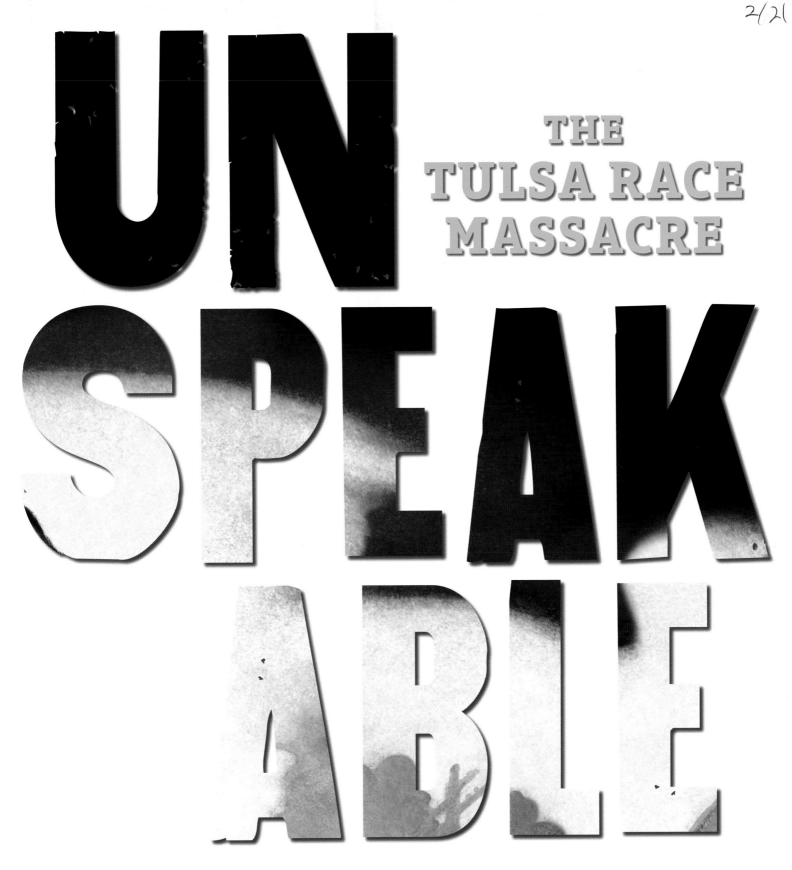

UNSPEAKABLE

THE TULSA RACE MASSACRE

CAROLE BOSTON WEATHERFORD · FLOYD COOPER

CAROLRHODA BOOKS
MINNEAPOLIS

2/21

Once upon a time near Tulsa, Oklahoma,

prospectors struck it rich in the oil fields.

The wealth created jobs, raised buildings,

and attracted newcomers from far and wide,

seeking fortune and a fresh start.

Once upon a time in Tulsa,

there was a community called Greenwood.

Its residents descended from Black Indians,

from formerly enslaved people, and from Exodusters,

who moved West in the late 1800s fleeing

the violence and racism of the segregated South.

Once upon a time in Greenwood,

there were some ten thousand people living

in a thirty-five-square-block area.

Train tracks divided the Black and white communities.

Segregation laws called for separate neighborhoods,

schools, phone booths, and railroad and streetcar coaches.

Unfair tests made it hard for Blacks to register to vote.

And laws barred marriages across racial lines.

So many Black businesses cropped up
along a one-mile stretch of Greenwood Avenue,
that educator and business leader Booker T. Washington
called the area the "Negro Wall Street of America."
The name later became Black Wall Street,
and the community kept thriving.

Once upon a time on Black Wall Street,

there were dozens of restaurants and grocery stores.

There were furriers, a pool hall, a bus system, and an auto shop—

nearly two hundred businesses in all.

There were also several libraries, a hospital,
a post office, and a separate school system,
where some say Black children
got a better education than whites.

There were two Black-owned newspapers—the *Tulsa Star*

and *Oklahoma Sun*—
and over twenty churches.

And fifteen Black doctors,
including Dr. A. C. Jackson,

the most able Black surgeon
in the nation.

On Detroit Avenue stood grand homes

of doctors, lawyers, and prominent businessmen.

Once upon a time in Greenwood,

there were barbershops and beauty salons.

Miss Mabel's Little Rose
Beauty Salon boomed

on Thursdays when maids
who worked for white families

got coiffed on their day off
and strutted in style

up and down
Greenwood Avenue.

The soda fountain
at Williams Confectionery

was the backdrop for scores
of marriage proposals.

And there was the luxurious Stradford Hotel,

then the largest Black-owned hotel in the nation.

Black guests were welcome there

even as they were barred from Tulsa's white hotels.

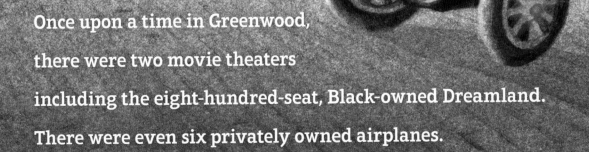

Once upon a time in Greenwood,

there were two movie theaters

including the eight-hundred-seat, Black-owned Dreamland.

There were even six privately owned airplanes.

But in 1921, not everyone in Tulsa was pleased

with these signs of Black wealth—undeniable proof

that African Americans could achieve

just as much, if not more than, whites.

All it took was one elevator ride,

one seventeen-year-old white elevator operator

accusing a nineteen-year old Black shoeshine man

of assault for simmering hatred to boil over.

With the accused man in jail,

the white-owned *Tulsa Tribune* newspaper

ran a headline prompting readers to "nab" him.

Fearing the man would be lynched—

killed by a mob before his trial—

thirty armed Black men rushed downtown to his rescue.

At the jail, they faced off with two thousand armed whites.

On May 31, 1921, one day after Memorial Day—

a holiday honoring fallen soldiers—

skirmishes between the two groups

left two Black men and ten white men dead.

But the worst was yet to come.

Unable to get to the jailed suspect,

the white mob sparked rumors

that the Black community planned to attack.

Unchecked and, in some cases, deputized by the police,

the white mob stormed into Greenwood,

looting and burning homes and businesses

that Blacks had saved and sacrificed to build.

Threatening to shoot, the mob blocked

firefighters from putting out the blazes.

African American World War I veterans

took up arms to defend their families and property.

But they were outnumbered and outgunned.

Families fled with only what they could carry.

Once upon a time in Greenwood,

up to three hundred Black people,
including Dr. Jackson, were killed.

Hundreds more were injured.
More than eight thousand people

were left homeless.
And hundreds of businesses

and other establishments
were reduced to ash.

The police did nothing to protect
the Black community.

When the National Guard arrived
the next day, all that was left to do

was put out fires and move
thousands of Black residents

into camps outside of Tulsa.
As their community lay in ruins,

Black residents had to carry
passes to enter the city.

In the days and weeks that followed,

some Black Tulsans left and never returned.

Others stayed and rebuilt the Greenwood community

only to witness its decline in the 1960s.

For decades, survivors did not speak of the terror.

Seventy-five years passed
before lawmakers launched

an investigation to uncover
the painful truth

about the worst racial attack
in United States history:

police *and* city officials had plotted
with the white mob

to destroy the nation's
wealthiest Black community.

Today, Tulsa's Reconciliation Park remembers victims
of the 1921 massacre and recalls the role
of African Americans in Oklahoma history.
But the park is not just a bronze monument to the past.
It is a place to realize the responsibility we all have
to reject hatred and violence and to instead choose hope.

AUTHOR'S NOTE

For me, racist backlash hits close to home. One cousin in Tennessee burned to death in his home, a rumored lynching. In the 1920s, whites allegedly burned down a store that belonged to another of my cousins in an all-Black village cofounded by my great-great-grandfather during Reconstruction. In my adopted state of North Carolina, another "Black Wall Street" anchored Durham, once a hub of Black enterprise. And another race massacre occurred—in Wilmington in 1898. Thus, family lore and proximity to history led me to the 1921 Tulsa Race Massacre.

Tulsa's history stretches back to 1836 when Muscogee (Creek) Indians who had been forced to leave Alabama settled there. The name Tulsa comes from the Creek word Tallasi, or Tvlvhasse, meaning "old town." At the time, what is now Oklahoma was part of an area known as Indian Territory, and other tribes in the Southeast were also forced to relocate there. In the decades that followed, increasing numbers of Blacks and whites moved to the area, and Oklahoma became a US state in 1907.

During the early twentieth century, Tulsa transformed into a booming oil town, and many African Americans viewed it as a promised land. Tulsa's thriving African American main street of Greenwood Avenue was even dubbed Black Wall Street. Yet many white Tulsans resented the success of the Black community.

Nationwide, racial tensions increased when World War I ended in 1918. African American soldiers who had fought and shed blood for their country hoped to receive greater respect back at home. But they did not. Violence against African Americans broke out in numerous cities and states in the summer of 1919, which became known as the Red Summer. Regardless of the supposed cause, the white mobs' motives were always to limit Black political and economic progress and to reassert white supremacy.

Then, on May 30, 1921, in Tulsa, Dick Rowland, an African American teen, either stumbled or stepped on the foot of Sarah Page, a young white elevator operator in a downtown office building. Page screamed, and the next day Rowland was jailed. A newspaper report that Rowland assaulted Page stoked existing racial tensions, inciting a white mob, initially numbering in the hundreds, that was bent on lynching the teen. Black men and boys were frequent victims of white lynch mobs that publicly murdered them, often by hanging, for alleged offenses. A smaller number of Black residents came to the courthouse where Rowland was being held in an effort to protect him. When the sheriff refused to surrender Rowland, the white mob, which had been increasing in number, turned violent. After a night of scattered attacks, at dawn the mob invaded the Black community, burning down at least 1,250 homes and two hundred businesses and robbing and looting hundreds more. The sixteen-hour massacre claimed countless lives. Among the dead was an African American boy shot in a movie theater. Many victims were buried in unmarked graves.

Even before the smoke had cleared, police dropped the charges against Dick Rowland, and he was released from jail. He left town the very next day, reportedly for good.

Exact numbers of fatalities, casualties, and participants are unknown because public officials at the time focused on covering up the massacre rather than

Top: Some African Americans fled by truck during the massacre.
Bottom: Smoke billowed over Tulsa as Greenwood burned.

documenting it. Not until the twenty-first century was this tragic chapter of history even taught in Oklahoma schools. In 1997 the State of Oklahoma authorized an investigation into the so-called race riot. The Oklahoma Commission to Study the Tulsa Race Riot of 1921 concluded that the violence left from 150 to 300 people dead and more than 8,000 people homeless.

In the wake of the massacre, Greenwood was rapidly rebuilt. Yet the burial sites of most of the massacre's Black victims have never been found. In July 2020, researchers excavated an area of Tulsa's Oaklawn Cemetery in an effort to locate unmarked mass graves, but they discovered no evidence of human remains.

In Greenwood today, you'll find John Hope Franklin Reconciliation Park. It includes a Tower of Reconciliation as well as three bronze sculptures based on photographs from the massacre representing hostility, humiliation, and hope. A world-class history center is currently being built, and other improvements to the Greenwood District are ongoing.

Above left: At John Hope Franklin Reconciliation Park, one of the three bronze sculptures shows a Black man with his hands raised in surrender in the aftermath of the massacre.
Above right: The Tower of Reconciliation depicts the history of African Americans in Oklahoma.

ILLUSTRATOR'S NOTE

The creation of this book started in 2018, but my connection to the story goes back to my childhood in Tulsa and visits to my grandpa in Muskogee. My grandpa *loved* to talk. When family came to visit, he talked. When a neighbor dropped by, right there on the front steps he'd go on for hours about history, current events, news, and politics. We kids thought this was soooo boring! But we hung around because we loved to hear Grandpa's voice, and every now and then we'd learn a few things.

Grandpa Williams circa 1940

In those days, not many people talked about what had happened back in 1921. But one night Grandpa talked about Greenwood. With us. He had grown up there, and he told us how he was home that night when folks from south of the Frisco tracks came into Greenwood. He said, "Everyone was caught off guard, like sitting ducks" when the looting, shooting, and fires burned Greenwood Avenue—the famous Black Wall Street—to the ground.

Everything I knew about this tragedy came from Grandpa; not a single teacher at school ever spoke of it.

For a long time, we knew it as the Tulsa Race Riot, but some people have said the word *riot* was just a way to further injure the Black community. Insurance companies didn't have to pay for damage to homes and businesses caused by a riot, so this meant Black folks had to find other ways to pay to rebuild what they'd lost. More recently, people have started calling it the Tulsa Race Massacre. A massacre is the violent killing of a number of usually helpless or unresisting people. By any name, it's an event that's deeply personal for me.

Now, the same way my grandpa told the story to us, I share it here with you. My grandpa passed away many years ago, but I hope that my art and Carole Boston Weatherford's words can speak for Grandpa.